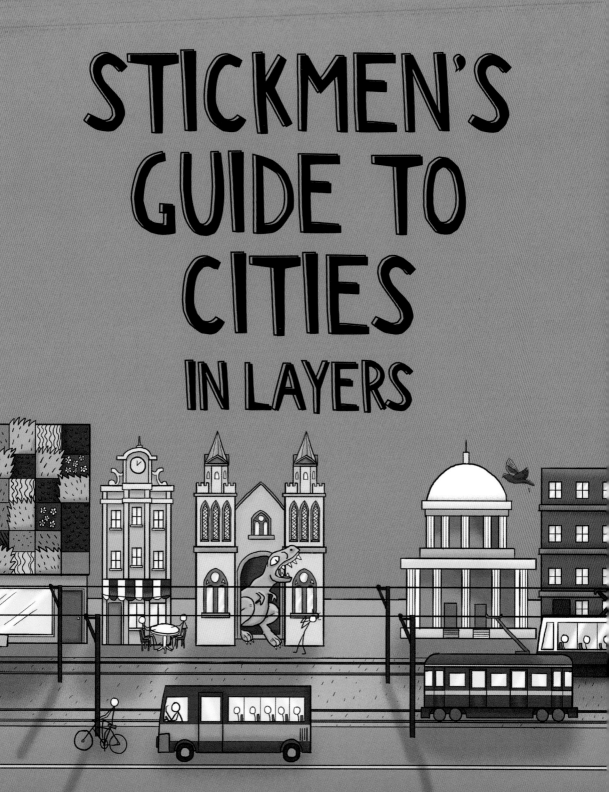

STICKMEN'S GUIDE TO CITIES
IN LAYERS

Thanks to the creative team:
Senior Editor: Alice Peebles
Fact checking: Kate Mitchell
Design: www.collaborate.agency

Hungry Tomato™
A division of Lerner Publishing Group, Inc.
241 First Avenue North
Minneapolis, MN 55401 USA

For reading levels and more information, look up this title at www.lernerbooks.com.

Main body text set in Avenir Next Medium 9.5/12. Typeface provided by Linotype AG.

Library of Congress Cataloging-in-Publication Data

Names: Chambers, Catherine, 1954- author. | Dean, Venitia, 1976- illustrator. | De Quay, John Paul, illustrator.
Title: Stickmen's guide to cities in layers / by Catherine Chambers ; illustrated by Venitia Dean, John Paul de Quay.
Description: Minneapolis : Hungry Tomato, [2017] | Series: Stickmen's guides to this incredible earth | Includes index.
Identifiers: LCCN 2015048779 (print) | LCCN 2016005021 (ebook) | ISBN 9781512406207 (lb : alk. paper) | ISBN 9781512411782 (pb : alk. paper) | ISBN 9781512409345 (eb pdf)
Subjects: LCSH: Urban geography—Juvenile literature. | Cities and towns—Juvenile literature.
Classification: LCC GF125 .C43 2017 (print) | LCC GF125 (ebook) | DDC 307.76—dc23

LC record available at http://lccn.loc.gov/2015048779

Manufactured in the United States of America
1 - VP - 7/15/16

STICKMEN'S GUIDE TO CITIES

IN LAYERS

by Catherine Chambers
Illustrated by John Paul de Quay

HUNGRY
TOMATO.

Contents

Cities

The most successful cities in the world attract millions of people. New arrivals and new businesses put pressure on land. This is why our biggest cities are built ever upwards—and down below ground level. This book takes a look at what happens from the very top to the underground depths, and the layers in between.

Reaching for the Sky
City skyscrapers soar higher and higher but no space is wasted, even at the top! The wind, sun, and great views are fully used.

High Power
From the top, elevators and escalators whisk you down from floor to floor, powered by electric cables hidden behind walls and ceilings.

Along the Ground
You can walk, cycle, or take the bus or streetcar along bustling city streets. Shiny store windows and dazzling neon lights make the big city sparkle.

Underground
For speedy travel, take a subway train. Also down under lie hidden networks of cabling and entire water and sewage systems.

On Top of the World

Architects test their skyscraper designs in wind tunnels to make sure the tops can cope with high winds. They build in curves and fins to reduce the impact. But they also make use of those dizzy heights and stiff breezes!

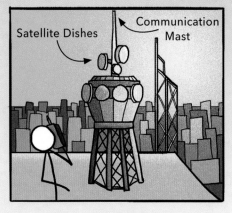

Satellite Dishes

Communication Mast

Getting the Message

Communications are key to running a city. Clear signals are vital, so the tops of skyscrapers are ideal sites for telecommunications equipment. These include antennae that receive radio waves, and transmitters that emit them. Sky-high satellite dishes receive signals from satellites orbiting Earth in the upper atmosphere.

Solar Panels

Soaking Up the Sun

The top of a tall building is the perfect place to capture the sun's energy. There are fewer tightly-packed buildings to create shadows. Here, panels of photovoltaic cells (solar panels) can be positioned to get maximum exposure to the sun all day. This is a sustainable way to make electricity.

Wind Turbine
Blades

Helipad
Landing
Target

Catching the Wind

This wind turbine at the top of a tower in Dubai is integrated into the building. Its clever design makes the turbine more stable in winds that can reach 93 miles per hour (150 kilometers per hour). Skyscrapers in many cities worldwide have to include a sustainable source of energy in their design, as shown here.

High Helipad

Flying in helicopters is a neat way of avoiding city traffic. More importantly, firefighters can land close to flames engulfing the tops of skyscrapers. The highest helipad sits on top of China's Guangzhou International Finance Center. Here, helicopters land 1,439 feet (438 meters) above the streets below.

Fun at the Top

Skyscrapers are expensive to build. Dubai's Burj Khalifa, the tallest building in the world, cost $1.5 billion. So investors and architects make sure that their rooftops are not wasted. They take full advantage of the view, if you dare look!

Parks in the Sky

There's a lot of luxury on top of modern skyscrapers. In Singapore, Marina Bay Sands Sky Park is a long 1,115-foot (340-m) entertainment space. It has 250 shade trees, a 492-foot (150-m) infinity swimming pool, and restaurants overlooking the South China Sea.

Sky Sports

Miniature golf courses, tennis courts, and running tracks can all be laid out on top of tall buildings, as this mini-golf course has been. Sky-high sports lovers might be surprised by an urban free-climber appearing suddenly over the railings. These extreme climbers use no safety gear to scale city skyscrapers.

Glass House with Arboretum

Miniature Golf

Infinity Pool

Flying Fairground

Hair-raising chair rides like this are suspended from skyscraper rooftops and rotate around them. Polercoaster, a new high-rise roller-coaster design, has a 5,200-foot (1,584-m) track that whizzes riders around at 65 miles per hour (100 km/h). It is due to open in 2017, on a retail complex in Orlando, Florida.

Greening the City

Plants grown on rooftop gardens help to absorb cities' polluting gases. They release more oxygen into the air for people to breathe, too.

Sheds on Top

High-rise roofs are not always topped by sleek restaurants and pools. Among air-conditioning vents and water tanks, some city dwellers build ramshackle sheds, sunrooms, greenhouses, vegetable garden beds, and even beehives. Some rooftops are planted with succulent species that need no artificial watering.

Air Conditioning Unit

Shed

Sunroom

Lawn

Flying Swings

Going Down...

Skyscrapers would be unusable without elevators to take you down from the top—or up from below. The lifts in China's new CTF Finance Center in Guangzhou city can descend at 65 feet (20 m) per second!

Elevators on the Edge

Elevators take up precious space inside narrow city buildings. So some are built on the outside, like this one on the Lloyds Building in London, United Kingdom.

Double-deckers

Skyscrapers can house thousands of people who line up at elevators during morning and evening rush hours. Double-decker elevators (left) that move both people and goods have helped solve the problem. They have two separate elevator cars in one unit, and stop at two floors at the same time. The first building to install these was the 110-story Sears Tower in Chicago, built in 1973. Engineers are now designing triple-decker elevators.

Carbon-fiber Cable

Counterweight (to stop car from falling out of control)

Cables often snapped with the first elevators, making the safety elevator very important.

Gate

Elevator Operator

Car

Super-cables

Tough steel cables raise and lower most elevators today. But superstrong, lightweight carbon-fiber cables and belts coated with tough polyurethane are being developed to replace them. Engineers are designing new braking systems to serve skyscrapers 3,300 feet (1,000 m) tall. Elevators can fall at 45 miles per hour (72 km/h)!

The First Elevator

Elevator design dates back to 236BCE in ancient Greece. But American Elisha Graves Otis introduced the first safety elevator in 1854. This was a spring-loaded device that caught the elevator platform should it fall. In the twentieth century, piston-powered hydraulic lifts were designed for low-rise buildings.

Testing, Testing

Engineers use computer simulation to design the lofty elevators of the future. But in Finland, the Kone company has plunged a 1,000-foot (305-m) test elevator shaft down into a limestone mine. Here, experimental elevators are tested at speeds of up to 56 feet (17 m) per second.

Hydraulic Elevator

Display with Floor Number

Car

Automatic Door

Shaft

Hydraulic Piston that Moves Elevator

Hydraulic Pump

Hydraulic Cylinder

High Power

Bright city lights that reach to the rooftops need constant power. So do vital safety systems, such as fire alarms, sprinklers, CCTV cameras, and security alarm systems. Offices need power and fiber-optic cables for computer and Internet links.

Patch Panel

High-wired

Electricians access patch panels between floors and ceilings to install and service power and communication hubs. These are connected to wiring threaded behind the walls.

The Largest Screen

Brightly lit screens advertising stores and shows dazzle high above city streets. New York City's Times Square boasts a screen that spans a whole block. It stretches from 45th to 46th Street, reaches eight stories high, and gleams with nearly 24 million LED (Light Emitting Diode) pixels.

Moore Lamp

Electricity Supply

Neon Gas or Liquid

Bright Lights

Tall buildings and narrow streets made cities very dark at night until about one hundred years ago. They lit up after Frenchman Georges Claude discovered that passing electricity through neon gas or liquid produced a bright red light. He confined the light inside a Moore Lamp, and the neon light was born.

LED Revolution

LEDs are bright spots of light produced by electricity, known as electroluminescence. They are often no bigger than a pinhead. Millions of these tiny red, green, and blue LED pixels together can create glowing multicolored images and words. They can move, too! LED bulbs are more energy-efficient than neon or fluorescent lights and are used to illuminate streets.

LED Bulbs

A Slice of Life

High-rise floors in the city can open up into vast workspaces. In department stores, internal escalators expose the whole space vertically. As customers travel up and down, they can take a snapshot view of each floor's displays and in-store advertising.

Endless Choices

In the 1880s, the first large department stores amazed their customers. Today, the biggest store is Shinsegae in Busan, South Korea, at more than 3.1 million square feet (288,000 square meters).

Ice Cream

Bear World!

Discount!

Computer-linked Work Hub

Easy Networking

Open-plan offices (left) allow easily linked work hubs, reducing the cost of installing and maintaining communications networks. Workers can communicate with each other quickly, and can be supervised closely. Many employees are now encouraged to personalize their work hubs so they do not all look the same.

The 1904 design of the Larkin Soap Company's office in the United States by Frank Lloyd Wright used the Taylorist Open Plan idea.

Early Open Plan

In the early 1900s, the number of office workers expanded, especially in mail-order firms, banks, and insurance companies. Efficient and bright office design was needed. So the American mechanical engineer, Frederick Winslow Taylor, created the "Taylorist Open Plan" concept. Workers were crammed together in a large space, performing small, repetitive tasks.

Floor Plan

Office Desk Position

Noisy Neighbors

Sound travels vertically between floors, but cavity flooring solutions reduce the problem. Square floor panels that rest on short columns allow a gap, or cavity, between the floor and the ceiling below. The gap absorbs loud sounds, and carpeting on top of it adds extra insulation.

Carpet to Dull Sound

Cavity Sound Insulation

On the Streets

Glamorous store windows, cosy cafés, and bustling sidewalks make the city's ground level a very attractive place. But pedestrians have to deal with cars, buses, streetcars, and bicycles streaming by. Noise and fumes fill the air in many large cities.

Living Wall

MUSEUM

Bicycle and Bus Lane

Living Walls

City pollution is a huge health problem. Walls of plants that absorb carbon gases from vehicles help clean the air and look great, too. France's Patrick Blanc, an artist and botanist, began this trend thirty years ago. The plants are rooted to soil held in mesh and are watered automatically.

Rattling Streetcars

Streetcars are trains on tracks powered by electrified overhead wires. First used in Russia in the 1880s, they are quieter and cleaner than motorized vehicles. They will be cleaner still when all streetcars use new wire-free supercapacitors. These are stores of electricity released to power the streetcars.

Quiet Tracks

Streetcar tracks clatter. So in some cities, grass is laid between the tracks to dampen the sound. The grass also absorbs pollution in the air. In the city of Rotterdam in the Netherlands, street surfaces are now made of a special asphalt that reduces vehicle noise.

Electrified Overhead Wires

MOVIE THEATER

Streetcar

Streetcar Track

Grass and Concrete Streetcar Track

BUS LANE

BUS LANE

Concrete Honeycomb Shapes with Porous Grass Pockets

Flood Danger

Heavy rain runs off the city's hard concrete and tarmac surfaces, filling drains and flooding streets. Grasscrete, openwork concrete paving with grass centers, allows water to soak in.

Power under Our Feet

Below the city streets, networks of cables bring light, heat, and communications to billions of people. Above ground, these wires would be exposed to snow, ice, and high winds. The first underground cabling was laid 150 years ago.

The Price of Power

Installing power below our streets can be dangerous work and disrupts busy pedestrians. It is also expensive. Underground electric cables cost between five and ten times more to install than those above ground. Repairing them can cost 60 percent more.

Bending Light

Office computers and cash registers operate by using signal transmitters called optical fibers. These thin tubes of high-quality glass carry information as light rays that seem to bend as they move, by bouncing along the tubes.

Thick Cladding

Glass Tube

Light Ray Reflecting as It Moves

Bundles of Optical Fibers

Laying Cables

Cables are pushed into position using rods, or pulled by winches. The jetting technique pushes cables through with a rush of air. This helps to stop them from sticking against pipes or other cables. Floating the cables in a stream of water prevents buckling and bending as they are fed through.

Cable Pushing Machine

Live Electricity Wire

Gnaw, Really?

When power is cut, engineers often find that the cable jackets have been gnawed through. This is the work of mice, rats, and gophers trying to sharpen their teeth! Solutions include a steel coating on the cables or treating them with capsaicin, a burning chemical found in chili peppers!

Cable Casing or Ducting

Digging Deep

Our growing cities need more and more cable networks. It means digging further down or expanding the tunnels that carry them. Engineers must then ensure that cables can take the increased pressure from above. They do this with heavy insulation, pipes, and ducting around the cables.

Keeping Clean

Deep underground, millions of gallons of water are pumped up into the city, where water is used in all kinds of ways and then drained away again. Underground sewage systems were first developed in the ancient cities of the Indus Valley (now in Pakistan) in 2500BCE.

Rising Water

In a flood, water gushes through sewers and up into the streets. Many cities are built on the coast or river floodplains, and are expanding. This puts pressure on both the water table (the underground water level) and pumps that carry away excess water. Excessive rainfall during torrential storms pushes a city's sewage system to its limits.

Facing Fatbergs

Fatbergs are huge balls of fat that slow the flow of our sewage systems. They solidify from cooking oils washed down millions of sinks. In 2013, a sewage worker in Kingston, United Kingdom, found a fatberg as big as two African elephants. It took up 95 percent of the sewer pipe.

Fatberg Containing Waste

Stop That Leak!

Leaking pipes in the water system are a costly waste. In the United States, $2.8 billion a year is spent fixing them. Water engineers access pipes through manhole covers set into sidewalks. They close shutoff valves between lengths of supply pipes to find which one is broken.

Manhole Cover

Shutoff Valve

Down the Plughole

In nineteenth-century industrial cities, people died because dirty water and poor sewage spread disease. It took until 1866 for London to have a clean system of sewers, designed by Joseph Bazalgette.

Sewage and Storm Drain System

Storm Drain

Wastewater from Factory

Sewage Treatment Plant

Treated Water Flowing Downstream

Wastewater from House

Sewer

Combined Sewer

Sanitary Waste and Storm Water

Overflow Structure

Precious Water

Cities are now installing more digital water and drainage meters. This makes people aware of the value of water, and how much they use. In 2015, nine cities in California were declared the United States' most drought-stricken.

Combined Sewer Outlet

Public Waterway

Travel below Ground

Underground subways help ease traffic jams and packed sidewalks in the streets above. One of the most modern is Copenhagen's subway, in Denmark, which runs twenty-fours hours with driverless trains.

Underground
Subway Station
Entrance

Double-decker Trains

At peak travel times, subway systems are now as packed as the streets above. Double-decker trains have been introduced to solve overcrowding problems in cities such as Berlin, Germany, and Sydney, Australia.

Escalator

Early Tunnel Boring Machine

Tunneling the Subways

The invention of hefty tunnel boring machines (TBMs) made it possible to carve out the first subway tunnel. Today's TBMs are surprisingly similar in design, but much longer, like a factory in a tube. In London, the new Crossrail subway system needed eight TBMs, each about as long as two Airbus 380 airliners. They dug down 131 feet (40 m) beneath the streets.

First Subway

In 1890, the City and South London Railway opened the world's first deep-level, electrified underground railway. A masterpiece of engineering, it ran from north to south London through a tunnel built under the River Thames. The locomotives were small enough to fit the narrow tunnels, and could haul three cars at speeds up to 25 miles per hour (40 km/h).

Subway Facts

Most Stations	New York, USA (422)
Most Lines	New York, USA (24)
Longest Track	Shanghai, China 334 miles (538 km)
Most Passengers	Beijing, China (more than 10 million a day)
Deepest Station	Ukraine, Kiev's Arsenalna station 351 feet (107 m)

Subway Station Entrance
Subway Lines
Subway Train at Platform
Junctions

Planning the Lines

Subway lines converging on a single station require careful planning. Junctions join lines as they approach a platform. Here, signals stop trains on different lines from accessing a platform at the same time. New lines weave through existing ones, avoiding sewers, power supplies, and underground rivers.

Down Under

Foundations reach down to the deepest layer of our cities. They support the increasing number and height of multi-story buildings. New foundation technologies allow construction on what was once seen as unstable, unsuitable land.

Caisson Pile

Steel Rod Reinforcement

Pile Walls Made of Steel

Floating Foundation

Bedrock

Soil

Sinking Feeling

Soft soils make normal foundations sink. But large, flat floating foundations that support high-rise buildings allow them just to shift slightly as the earth gives way. Clay is a soft soil but only when wet. When dry, it shrinks, causing buildings above to subside. So deep supporting piles are driven below the clay.

Pushing Down Piles

Tall buildings are held up by long supports called piles, which are driven by machinery into the bedrock. Caissons are massive cylindrical piles reinforced by steel rods. They are at least 3 feet 3 inches (1 m) in diameter. Steel sheet pile walls help keep soil and rubble around them from shifting.

Deepest Foundations

Malaysia's Petronas Twin Towers soar 1,483 feet (452 m) above street level. They are so tall that their pinnacles house aircraft warning lights. They sit on foundations of reinforced concrete held up by 104 supporting rods, or piles. Some of these reach down 374 feet (114 m) and are the deepest in the world.

Hitting Water

The water table is the natural level of water beneath us. In many cities, foundations that are in contact with the water table push the level up. On construction sites, pumps remove excess water constantly. The basements of buildings can then be built from concrete encased by steel as a barrier to water.

Rocking with the Shock

Buildings set on rigid foundations crack in an earthquake. So new skyscrapers are designed to rock with the shock waves. They rest on foundations fitted with isolators, or flexible pads, that lift the buildings above the ground and allow them to lean. At the top of the building, a heavy weight swings in a harness to rebalance the structure if it lurches too much to one side.

Steel Bracing for Strength

Foundation's Isolator

Fantastic City Facts

High-rise Hong Kong

Hong Kong, in southeast China, has an amazing 1,268 skyscrapers, with more being built all the time. New York has 684, the second largest number. Hong Kong is a bustling commercial city built on a small island and islets in the Pearl River delta. It spreads outward on reclaimed land, but building upward is still vital to the city's prosperity.

Top Tennis

In 2005, tennis stars Andrei Agassi of the United States and Switzerland's Roger Federer played a match high on a helipad—atop Dubai's Burj al Arab hotel, 689 feet (210 m) in the air. The tennis court lies within the helipad's circle, which juts out below the top of this 1,053-foot (321-m) tall hotel.

One Large Plan

In 2015, the Facebook offices moved into the largest open plan office in the world, in Menlo Park, California. It was designed to house 3,400 engineers, all working in the same space, though there are smaller, quiet areas, too. The roof dips and rises like a wave, 45-73 feet (14-22 m) above ground, with trees planted on the top.

Triple Elevators

Engineers have designed a triple-decker elevator to take people up and down the new wave of super-skyscrapers. They are so tall that they have to stop at two floors at a time. Designers need to reduce the weight of these elevators and their ropes and pulleys to allow them to move—and fast!

City Cycling

Down at street level, cyclists compete with streetcars and traffic. But things are not so bad for cyclists in Copenhagen, Denmark. Here, there are more than 242 miles (390 km) of cycle track. Copenhagen is regularly voted the best bike city in the world. In winter, cycle tracks are cleared of snow before roads. Bikes rule!

Time at the Top

If you need to know the time in the city of Makkah, Saudi Arabia, just look up at the Royal Clocktower Hotel, in the Abraj al-Bait complex. This four-sided clock is 1,972 feet (601 m) high and can be seen 15 miles (25 km) away.

Tallest Living Wall

The living wall growing inside the Desjardins office building in Levis, Quebec, in Canada, rises 213 feet (65 m) inside a glass atrium. It has eleven thousand plants with forty-two different species, including ginger, fig trees, and banana plants. They are not rooted in soil, but are fed with water containing nutrients.

Snake in the Sewers

In 2015, in Manchester, United Kingdom, a snake kept popping up in bathrooms from deep in the sewers. Fiber-optic equipment was fed underground, but the snake was nowhere to be seen. Finally, the 10-foot (3-m) boa constrictor was spotted again in a bathroom and caught in a bucket. Its name was Keith.

The Future...

More and more people are living in cities and the only way they can expand is up—and down. In the future they might look like layers of streets in the sky. Buildings might reach so high that the air is too thin to breathe outside them.

New Designs

Most tall city buildings taper at the top. This affects the way they are used, with department stores or car parking spaces at the bottom, and offices and apartments at the thinner peaks. New mushroom-shaped designs are allowing greater, more versatile space in the upper layers.

Night Sky

Light pollution prevents city dwellers from enjoying a dark, starlit sky that is highly visible in the coutryside. Street lamps with new LED bulbs use less energy and glow with a softer light, which is filtered to reduce glare. Hooded shades point light beams down, improving the quality of the darkness in the city.

Windy Cities

Increased wind speeds and flooding may threaten safety in our cities. Engineers and architects are designing materials and structures that can withstand them. Tall buildings add to the problem of wind by creating a downdraft. In a cyclone, wind traveling between high-rise structures creates a fast-spinning vortex.

New Ways of Living

Maybe in the future there will be so many city dwellers that they will occupy high-rise layers connected by walkways and cycleways. Or they will live underground. Architects are designing skyscrapers made of shipping containers as temporary housing. And in cities near the sea, such as Lagos, Nigeria, new artificial islands are being created for people to live and work on.

Glossary

asphalt:
building material made of stones and fillers bound with tar

carbon fiber:
strengthening material made of fine carbon threads

cavity:
gap or space

grasscrete:
concrete mosaic with patches of grass that allow for water drainage

insulation:
material or space that keeps in sound or heat

isolator:
support that allows a building above to move

junction:
where two lines meet

manhole cover:
strong cast iron entrance to underground storm drains and sewers

neon:
gas or liquid that makes a colored light when electricity passes through it

orbiting:
circling an object

patch panel:
square unit that can be opened up to install or fix equipment behind it

photovoltaic cell:
cell that can convert energy from the sun into electricity

pile:
long, strong rod that holds up a building

polyurethane:
strong plastic material

spring-loaded:
spring that presses one part against another part

supercapacitor:
quick-charging electricity store that uses static electricity

succulent:
fleshy-leaved plant that needs little watering

INDEX

The Author

Catherine Chambers was born in Adelaide, South Australia, grew up in the United Kingdom, and studied African History and Swahili at the School of Oriental and African Studies in London. She has written close to 130 books for children and young adults, and enjoys seeking out intriguing facts for her nonfiction titles, which cover history, cultures, faiths, biography, geography, and the environment.

The Illustrator

John Paul de Quay has a BSc in Biology from the University of Sussex, United Kingdom, and a graduate certificate in animation from the University of the West of England. He devotes his spare time to growing chili peppers, perfecting his plan for a sustainable future, and caring for a small plastic dinosaur. He has three pet squid that live in the bath, which makes drawing in ink quite economical . . .